Time Tests

Take the Challenge

Percentages

by Norman D Lock
cover illustration by Gary Slater

Published by Flying Frog Publishing,
an imprint of Allied Publishing Group, Inc.

Test 1

1	7
2	× 3
3	add nine
4	÷ 2
5	divide by three
6	square it
7	double it
8	4 extra
9	÷ 9
10	multiply by three

What is your answer?

Check your answer at the back of the book.

Record your time on the Record Sheet.

Test 2

1	$5
2	times 8
3	half of this
4	half of this
5	$8 more
6	split equally between two
7	× 5
8	+ $5
9	$\frac{1}{2}$ of this
10	$\frac{1}{2}$ of this

What is your answer?

Check your answer at the back of the book.

Record your time on the Record Sheet.

Test 3

1	six
2	square it
3	÷ 4
4	times 3
5	minus three
6	split into 6 equal parts
7	× 8
8	add ten
9	divide by 7
10	multiply by 8

What is your answer?
Check your answer at the back of the book.
Record your time on the Record Sheet.

Test 4

1	$12
2	÷ 3
3	increase by $3
4	8 groups of this amount
5	split equally among 7 people
6	remove $3
7	× 7
8	double this amount
9	subtract $15
10	÷ 5

What is your answer?
Check your answer at the back of the book.
Record your time on the Record Sheet.

Test 5

Percentages are simply a type of fraction.

The symbol used for percentages is %. This stands for 'per cent' which means 'out of a hundred'.

So:

50% means $\frac{50}{100} = \frac{1}{2}$

25% means $\frac{25}{100} = \frac{1}{4}$

75% means $\frac{75}{100} = \frac{3}{4}$

$33\frac{1}{3}$% is equivalent to $\frac{1}{3}$

$66\frac{2}{3}$% is equivalent to $\frac{2}{3}$

* Learn these by heart so that you can use them very quickly.

1	$8
2	4 groups of this
3	50% of this
4	find 25%
5	× 9
6	add $4
7	25% of this
8	find 50%
9	× 6
10	50% of this

What is your answer?

Check your answer at the back of the book.

Record your time on the Record Sheet.

Test 6

1	36
2	find the square root
3	× 8
4	find 50%
5	50% of this
6	find 25%
7	times 9
8	add 13
9	75% of this
10	find $33\frac{1}{3}$%

What is your answer?

Check your answer at the back of the book.

Record your time on the Record Sheet.

Test 7

1	$20
2	75% of this
3	find $33\frac{1}{3}$%
4	multiply by 9
5	subtract $3
6	50% of this
7	find $66\frac{2}{3}$%
8	÷2
9	× 4
10	find 50%

What is your answer?

Check your answer at the back of the book.

Record your time on the Record Sheet.

Test 8

1	seven
2	square it
3	eleven more
4	$66\frac{2}{3}\%$ of this
5	find 25%
6	× 8
7	plus one
8	find the square root
9	$33\frac{1}{3}\%$ of this
10	multiply by 8

What is your answer?

Check your answer at the back of the book.

Record your time on the Record Sheet.

Test 9

1	$24
2	$66\frac{2}{3}\%$ of this
3	find 75%
4	50% of this
5	× 6
6	double it
7	divide by 9
8	25% of this
9	multiply by 7
10	double it

What is your answer?

Check your answer at the back of the book.

Record your time on the Record Sheet.

10% means $\frac{10}{100} = \frac{1}{10}$

As you know, to find $\frac{1}{10}$ of something you divide by 10. There is a quick way of doing this. Look at these examples:

H T 1's
4 0 ÷ 10
= 4

H T 1's
3 5 0 ÷ 10
= 3 5

The numbers move **one** place to the right. We can do the same with money.

10% of \$12 or $\frac{1}{10}$ of \$12
$\$12.00 \div 10 = \$1.20$

10% of \$3.70 or $\frac{1}{10}$ of \$3.70
$\$3.70 \div 10 = \$0.37$
(or 37 cents)

10% of 90 cents or $\frac{1}{10}$ of 90 cents
$\$0.90 \div 10 = \$0.09$
(or 9 cents)

1	fifty
2	find 10%
3	× 4
4	seven extra
5	$33\frac{1}{3}\%$ of this
6	square it
7	remove eleven
8	50% of this
9	- 15
10	10% of this

What is your answer?

Check your answer at the back of the book.

Record your time on the Record Sheet.

Test 11

1	$32
2	deduct $7
3	find 10%
4	double it
5	add $4
6	10% of this
7	5 groups of this
8	double it
9	double it
10	10% of this

What is your answer?
Check your answer at the back of the book.
Record your time on the Record Sheet.

Test 12

1	$100
2	find 75%
3	minus $3
4	find 50%
5	÷ 9
6	10% of this
7	× 5
8	25% of this
9	find 50%
10	÷ 5

What is your answer?
Check your answer at the back of the book.
Record your time on the Record Sheet.

Test 13

1	$150
2	find 10%
3	$33\frac{1}{3}\%$ of this
4	× 6
5	subtract $9
6	find $66\frac{2}{3}\%$
7	50% of this
8	find 10%
9	times 4
10	10% of this

What is your answer?

Check your answer at the back of the book.

Record your time on the Record Sheet.

Test 14

1	900
2	50% of this
3	find 10%
4	÷ 9
5	+ 3
6	square it
7	75% of this
8	÷ 6
9	add 22
10	10% of this

What is your answer?

Check your answer at the back of the book.

Record your time on the Record Sheet.

Test 15

Now that you know how to find 10%, finding 20%, 30% 40%, etc. is easy.

For example, **30% is 3 groups of 10%.**

Find 30% and 70% of $9:
10% is $\frac{1}{10}$ of $9.00, so

10% is $0.90

30% is 3 x $0.90 = $2.70
(3 groups of 9 dimes, which is 27 dimes = $2.70)

70% is $\frac{7}{10}$ of $9.00

70% is 7 x $0.90 = $6.30

For 20%, 40%, 60% and 80% you can also use another method.

$20\% = \frac{20}{100} = \frac{2}{10} = \frac{1}{5}$

$40\% = \frac{40}{100} = \frac{4}{10} = \frac{2}{5}$

$60\% = \frac{60}{100} = \frac{6}{10} = \frac{3}{5}$

$80\% = \frac{80}{100} = \frac{8}{10} = \frac{4}{5}$

For example, to find 60% of $15 you could use:

Method 1:

10% of $15.00 = $1.50
60% is 6 x $1.50 = $9.00

or **Method 2:**

60% is $\frac{3}{5}$

$\frac{1}{5}$ of $15.00 = $3.00

$\frac{3}{5}$ or 60% = 3 x $3.00
              = $9.00

1	forty
2	find 30%
3	double it
4	+ 1
5	find the square root
6	times 7
7	double it
8	20% of this
9	find 50%
10	square it

What is your answer?
Check your answer at the back of the book.
Record your time on the Record Sheet.

Test 16

1	$20
2	90% of this
3	add $16
4	find 50%
5	deduct $10
6	40% of this
7	minus $2
8	find 25%
9	x 5
10	find 70%

What is your answer?

Check your answer at the back of the book.

Record your time on the Record Sheet.

Test 17

1	ten
2	square it
3	+ 21
4	find the square root
5	times 5
6	remove 5
7	find 80%
8	75% of this
9	find 50%
10	multiply by four

What is your answer?

Check your answer at the back of the book.

Record your time on the Record Sheet.

Test 18

1	$30
2	60% of this
3	find $33\frac{1}{3}$%
4	x 9
5	plus $6
6	80% of this
7	find 75%
8	10% of this
9	deduct $3
10	times 7

What is your answer?
Check your answer at the back of the book.
Record your time on the Record Sheet.

Test 19

1	five hundred
2	find 40%
3	50% of this
4	find the square root
5	70% of this
6	square it
7	seven more
8	divide by 8
9	x 10
10	find 30%

What is your answer?
Check your answer at the back of the book.
Record your time on the Record Sheet.

Test 20

1	$50
2	find 60%
3	80% of this
4	find $66\frac{2}{3}$%
5	+ $12
6	divide equally into 4 parts
7	× 9
8	$3 less than this
9	find 90%
10	÷ 6

What is your answer?

Check your answer at the back of the book.

Record your time on the Record Sheet.

Test 21

1	$12
2	20% of this
3	add 10 cents
4	double it
5	find 40%
6	30% of this
7	multiply by 7
8	80 cents extra
9	× 8
10	70% of this

What is your answer?

Check your answer at the back of the book.

Record your time on the Record Sheet.

Test 22

1% means:
1 out of a hundred = $\frac{1}{100}$

To find $\frac{1}{100}$ of something you divide by 100. There is a quick way of doing this. When you divided by 10, you moved the numbers **one** place to the right.

When you divide by 100, move them **two** places to the right.

Look at these examples:

$$\begin{array}{ccc} H & T & U \\ 7 & 0 & 0 \end{array} \div 100$$
$$= \rightarrow \rightarrow 7$$

$$\begin{array}{cccc} Th & H & T & U \\ 5 & 6 & 0 & 0 \end{array} \div 100$$
$$= \rightarrow \rightarrow 5\ 6$$

Here are some money ones:
1% of \$27 or $\frac{1}{100}$ of \$27
  \$27.00 ÷ 100
  = \$>>.27
    (or 27 cents)

1% of \$6 or $\frac{1}{100}$ of \$6
  \$6.00 ÷ 100
  = \$0.06
    (or 6 cents)

1% of \$134 or $\frac{1}{100}$ of \$134
  \$134.00 ÷ 100
  = \$>>1.34
    (or \$1.34 cents)

1	six hundred
2	1 % of this
3	× 9
4	subtract 14
5	find 10%
6	× 7
7	increase by 2
8	50% of this
9	find $66\frac{2}{3}$ %
10	square it

What is your answer?
Check your answer at the back of the book.
Record your time on the Record Sheet.

Test 23

1	$25
2	find 1%
3	4 groups of this
4	x 13
5	add $27
6	double it
7	60% of this
8	find 1%
9	÷ 4
10	50% of this

What is your answer?

Check your answer at the back of the book.

Record your time on the Record Sheet.

Test 24

1	$7
2	70% of this
3	plus 10 cents
4	x 10
5	find 1%
6	times 8
7	multiply by 9
8	double it
9	$28 extra
10	1%

What is your answer?

Check your answer at the back of the book.

Record your time on the Record Sheet.

Test 25

1	50
2	× 6
3	1% of this
4	multiply by 9
5	double it
6	add 16
7	find 40%
8	divide by 7
9	times 9
10	$33\frac{1}{3}$% of this

What is your answer?

Check your answer at the back of the book.

Record your time on the Record Sheet.

Test 26

1	$60
2	find 75%
3	double it
4	1% of this
5	× 7
6	add 70 cents
7	times 8
8	find 1%
9	÷ 7
10	multiply by 9

What is your answer?

Check your answer at the back of the book.

Record your time on the Record Sheet.

If yo
ther
2%,

For
3% i

...u can find 1% ($\frac{1}{100}$),
...it is easy to find
...%, 4%, etc.

...xample
...3 groups of 1%.

...ind 3% of $7:

1% is $\frac{1}{100}$ of $7.00

1%   = $0.07
         (or 7 cents)

3% is 3 x 7 cents = $0.21
            (or 21 cents)

Another example:

Find 7% of $12:

1% of $12.00 = $0.12
            (or 12 cents)

7% is 7 x 12 cents = $0.84
            (or 84 cents)

To find 5% you can either
use the method shown
above or find 10% (which
is easy to do) and then
halve it.

Look at these:

Find 5% of $9:

10% of $9.00 = $0.90
            (or 90 cents)

5% is half of 90 cents = $0.45
            (or 45 cents)

Find 5% of $24:

10% of $24.00 = $2.40

5% is half of $2.40
         = $1.20

1	$5
2	find 3%
3	x 4
4	double it
5	double it
6	double it
7	add 20 cents
8	times 8
9	5% of this
10	75% of this

What is your answer?
Check your answer at the
back of the book.
Record your time on the
Record Sheet.

Test 28

1	200
2	find 8%
3	÷2
4	square it
5	plus 6
6	50% of this
7	take off 10
8	find the square root
9	x 100
10	11% of this

What is your answer?

Check your answer at the back of the book.

Record your time on the Record Sheet.

Test 29

1	$27
2	$33\frac{2}{3}$% of this
3	find 4%
4	6 cents more
5	split into 6 equal parts
6	100 times this
7	x 9
8	an additional $7
9	5% of this
10	50% of this

What is your answer?

Check your answer at the back of the book.

Record your time on the Record Sheet.

Test 30

1	$9
2	find 6%
3	take away 5 cents
4	split into 7 equal parts
5	× 9
6	double it
7	remove 1 cent
8	double it
9	20% of this
10	multiply by 7

What is your answer?

Check your answer at the back of the book.

Record your time on the Record Sheet.

Test 31

1	one thousand
2	8% of this
3	minus 16
4	find the square root
5	× 90
6	add 80
7	find 7%
8	50% of this
9	75% of this
10	$66\frac{2}{3}$% of this

What is your answer?

Check your answer at the back of the book.

Record your time on the Record Sheet.

Test 32

In this book, you have learned a quick way to **divide** by 10 and 100.

To divide by 10 you move the numbers **one** place to the **right** to make the number smaller:

$15   ÷ 10 or -
$15.00 ÷ 10
= $>1.50

To divide by 100 you move the numbers **two** places to the **right**.

$35   ÷ 100 or
$35.00 ÷ 100
= $>>.35
    (or 35 cents)

To multiply by 10 you move the numbers **one** place to the **left**.

36 cents x 10
$0.36 x 10
= $3.60
$1.95 x 10
= $19.50

To multiply by 100 you move the numbers **two** places to the **left**.

    5 cents x 100
$0.05 x 100
= $5.00

$2.75 x 100
= $275.00

1	7 cents
2	x 100
3	50% of this
4	x 10
5	÷ 7
6	find 10%
7	multiply by 6
8	1% of this
9	times 9
10	double it

What is your answer?

Check your answer at the back of the book.

Record your time on the Record Sheet.

Test 33

1	$2.70
2	x 10
3	divide by 9
4	multiply by 8
5	25% of this
6	find 5%
7	x 7
8	times 10
9	$9 added on
10	6% of this

What is your answer?
Check your answer at the back of the book.
Record your time on the Record Sheet.

Test 34

1	15 cents
2	x 100
3	double it
4	$6 extra
5	split into 9 equal parts
6	multiply by 100
7	75% of this
8	find 50%
9	$66\frac{2}{3}$% of this
10	find 3%

What is your answer?
Check your answer at the back of the book.
Record your time on the Record Sheet.

Test 35

1	28 cents
2	times by 10
3	25% of this
4	9 groups of this
5	find 10%
6	divide by 7
7	× 100
8	6 times this
9	add $6
10	find 2%

What is your answer?
Check your answer at the back of the book.
Record your time on the Record Sheet.

Test 36

1	$50
2	find 70%
3	double it
4	1% of this
5	× 8
6	remove 60 cents
7	find 50%
8	30% of this
9	double it
10	double it

What is your answer?
Check your answer at the back of the book.
Record your time on the Record Sheet.

You often see percentages written on signs in shop windows, especially during sales, to tell you that certain items are reduced in price.

For example, you might have seen "10% off all computer games" or "25% off the price of a television".

This is easy to work out.

Look at these examples:

A computer game normally costs $50. During the sale it is reduced in price by 10%. What does it now cost?

10% of $50 = $5
$50 minus $5 = $45
It now costs $45.

A television normally costs $240. During a sale it is reduced in price by 25%. What does it now cost?

25% of $240 = $60
$240 minus $60 = $180
It now costs $180.

1	$10
2	take away 10%
3	× 5
4	add $9
5	divide by 6
6	$33\frac{1}{3}\%$ of this
7	find 1%
8	times 50
9	double it
10	× 20

What is your answer?

Check your answer at the back of the book.

Record your time on the Record Sheet.

Test 38

1	$20
2	minus 25%
3	1% of this
4	× 4
5	double it
6	find 10%
7	multiply by four
8	× 100
9	add $2
10	7% of this

What is your answer?

Check your answer at the back of the book.

Record your time on the Record Sheet.

Test 39

1	$36
2	$33\frac{1}{3}$% of this
3	÷ 6
4	9% of this
5	double it
6	times 10
7	minus 20 cents
8	× 8
9	find 1%
10	divide by 7

What is your answer?

Check your answer at the back of the book.

Record your time on the Record Sheet.

Test 40

1	$80
2	find 75%
3	minus 10%
4	÷6
5	multiply by 5
6	10% of this
7	minus $2
8	3 times this
9	find 10%
10	double it

What is your answer?
Check your answer at the back of the book.
Record your time on the Record Sheet.

Test 41

1	3 cents
2	× 100
3	multiply by 6
4	$66\frac{2}{3}$% of this
5	find 10%
6	50% of this
7	times 7
8	add 80 cents
9	take away 10%
10	divide by 9

What is your answer?
Check your answer at the back of the book.
Record your time on the Record Sheet.

Test 42

Unfortunately you sometimes have to pay extra! Instead of having 10% off the price, sometimes you have to **add** a certain percentage.

Here are two examples: A meal costs $25 plus a 15% service charge. What is the full cost of the meal?

$$\begin{array}{r} \$25.00 \\ +15\% \quad \$3.75 \\ \hline \$28.75 \end{array}$$

The total bill is $28.75

Some furniture costs $400 and there is a 2% delivery charge. What is the full cost?

1% of $400 = $4

$$\begin{array}{r} \$400.00 \\ + 2\% \quad \$8.00 \\ \hline \$408.00 \end{array}$$

The total cost is $408.

1	$40
2	plus 10%
3	25% of this
4	take away $2
5	× 7
6	minus $3
7	10% off
8	÷ 6
9	find $33\frac{1}{3}\%$
10	multiply by 7

What is your answer?

Check your answer at the back of the book.

Record your time on the Record Sheet.

Test 43

1	$64
2	shared equally among 8 people
3	75% of this
4	× 10
5	double it
6	double it
7	deduct $30
8	find $66\frac{2}{3}\%$
9	50% of this
10	add 5%

What is your answer?

Check your answer at the back of the book.

Record your time on the Record Sheet.

Test 44

1	$500
2	plus 4%
3	+ $20
4	10% of this
5	divide by 9
6	find 1%
7	times 8
8	double it
9	4 cents extra
10	plus 9%

What is your answer?

Check your answer at the back of the book.

Record your time on the Record Sheet.

Test 45

1	23 cents
2	x 100
3	take away $9
4	2% of this
5	double it
6	times 10
7	divide by 7
8	times 100
9	plus 10%
10	75% of this

What is your answer?
Check your answer at the back of the book.
Record your time on the Record Sheet.

Test 46

1	$5000
2	3% of this
3	find 50%
4	take away $3
5	÷ 8
6	x 6
7	1% of this
8	add 6 cents
9	times 100
10	plus 30%

What is your answer?
Check your answer at the back of the book.
Record your time on the Record Sheet.

Record Sheet

Date	Test No.	Time	Score

Record Sheet

Date	Test No.	Time	Score

Record Sheet

Date	Test No.	Time	Score

Record Sheet

Date	Test No.	Time	Score